THE BUSINESS TEXT MESSAGE CONNECTION

How to Take Advantage Of SMS Marketing

Dwayne Whiting

Queen City Creations

CONTENTS

CHAPTER 1

TEXTING A SHORT HISTORY

A short 20 years ago, cell phone engineers scoffed at the idea of text messaging. Who would want to send a written message when they could just call on the phone? It seems public demand won over the engineers' doubts, and texting is here to stay.

It's said that the first text message was sent via pager in 1989 by Raina Forteni: the string of numbers 07734, which, when her friend turned the pager upside down, read "HELLO." True text messaging between cell phones didn't start happening until the mid-1990s, and it's only been since 2007 that a majority of mobile users are sending texts.

Americans (especially Americans between the ages of 12 and 24) might not believe it, but the United States wasn't the first nation to adopt broad cell phone texting. Sweden and Luxembourg led the way in the late 1990s; U.S. cell phone usage and text messaging numbers took over the world simply because of population numbers around 2009, when Americans sent about 152.7 billion texts per month.

SMS (Short Message Service) texts are familiar to most people today. SMS limits the number of characters sent and breaks messages into parts to deliver to the destination. The 160-character limit is actually arbitrary and doesn't really affect the service; SMS was originally standardized to 160 characters because engineers felt an average sentence was 160 characters long.

As mobile devices become smarter, it's easier to send text messages. Some phones have keyboards, which allow users to type in letters—much simpler than punching numbers several times to arrive at the correct letter. It's possible to chat from computer to cell phone now, too, so text messaging is even easier when two technologies are used at the same time.

When SMS became available in 1995, users sent less than one message per month via the service. Cell phone providers were slow to add the capability to cell phone plans, and texts were incredibly expensive to send and receive.

Perhaps the biggest reason for the explosion in texting stems from cell phone providers offering unlimited plans. Previously, there was a small charge per message—which could add up quickly if the user didn't stop to think about costs. Many families with teenagers have gotten a nasty surprise in the mail when the cell phone bill arrived.

Even though unlimited plans make it cheaper for individuals to send texts, the telecom industry still earns $114.6 billion per year on text messages. In 2010, mobile users sent about 192,000 texts per second worldwide.

Texting is definitely part of worldwide culture now. If you don't send text messages, you're in the distinct minority of cell phone users.

Texting: Mishaps

Oh, the many funny ways people can make mistakes with text messages!

Uh-Oh, Autocorrect!

The advent of "autocorrect" by most cell providers has led to some amusing and confusing verbal mishaps. Entire websites are devoted to making fun of unintentional—but correctly spelled—words, which change the entire context of the message.

In a recent news story, the autocorrect function changed a word and triggered a school lockdown. A Florida teenage boy texted, "gunna be at west hall today" and his phone sent, "gunman be at west hall today" to the wrong person. After the recipient panicked and called the police, all area schools were locked down until the unintentional message was sorted out.

Cell phone users can turn the autocorrect function off, and simply watch their spelling to avoid being the butt of a joke. Unfortunately, that requires people to pay attention to their spelling... So the amusing confusion may not be less, after all.

Oops! Wrong Number

It's incredibly easy to get people mixed up when sending texts to multiple numbers. If you're carrying on a conversation with your coworker and your spouse or partner at the same time, you'll need to watch the flirty language and inside jokes. Almost everyone has an embarrassing story of texting the wrong person the wrong message.

It should seem obvious, but you should enter full names in your cell phone's contact list and then double check yourself when you're sending messages. While most mix ups are innocent, there's no need to shock the babysitter or your mother with your racy words.

When celebrities have texting mishaps that go public, they can be shocking and funny. Lady Gaga mixed up her friend Anna Treblin with Anna Wintour, editor of Vogue Magazine, and called the wrong Anna a bitch. One has to wonder why Lady Gaga would call her friend a bitch, but that's another story.

And Then There's Sexting... Movie stars, pro athletes, singers and politicians have fallen victim to thinking their text messages are private conversations. The spirals of cheating can quickly get out of control, and affairs via text message are preserved in the phone until the cheater is revealed.

While the news media might make a big deal out of a famous person texting naked pictures to his mistress, ordinary people have also gotten into trouble with sexting. It's becoming more prevalent among teenagers, too, and then naughty text messages are no longer funny.

It's possible that the worst texting mishap is breaking up via text message. When it's time for a relationship to end, do it in per- son and take your lumps. If you must text to break up, just be sure it's to the right number and you've carefully checked your spelling.

Texting: How to Stay Safe

There are bright sides and dark sides to texting. Positive aspects of sending text messages include keeping up with friends and family in the various activities they do throughout the day; communicating even when cell phone signal strength is weak or it's impossible to make a call; and the convenience factor of having those messages stored in the phone until they're erased.

Texting has even become such a part of modern culture that there's an interesting push among U.S. law enforcement departments: receiving 911 calls via text message. This idea is modeled after the U.K. emergency system, wherein registered mobile users are allowed to make 911 calls via text. Not all U.S. regions have adopted this policy; call your local police to find out if your area responds to texted 911 calls.

There are plenty of negative things to say about texting, too. Here are a few tips to stay safe around text messages:

Set boundaries for yourself and your kids around texting. Parents should model good behavior and follow the same rules as kids.

Don't text and drive. Your risk of being involved in an accident is 23 times greater than when you're paying attention to the road. In fact, texting is more distracting than being drunk!

Protect your reputation by not sending sexually explicit texts or photos. Anything and everything done with technology has the possibility of becoming public.

If you have kids, watch out for bullying via text message. Nasty messages can be hurtful, and parents should be on the lookout for signs of bullying.

If you receive an obnoxious text from someone else, just delete it and don't respond. This may be hard for kids, especially if a so- called friend is sending obnoxious messages.

Be respectful of what other people might be doing when you send them text messages. Texting seems immediate, but others can't always respond immediately.

Think about your health. A formerly-rare type of tendonitis (tenosynovitis) has become a frequent complain among texters. It's caused by small repetitive movements of the thumb as the sufferer sends repeated text messages.

Overall, texting is a good way for everyone to keep in touch. As with any other technology, overuse can be harmful. It's always a good idea to put the cell phone away and participate in what's going on around you in a particular moment—paying attention could be critical for your health.

Texting: The Law

The explosive adoption of SMS messaging has left lawmakers scrambling to keep up. Dozens of court cases involving texting have popped up as law enforcement attempts to apply the usual standards to text messages or the act of texting.

Texting and Decency Laws

If a teenage girl snaps a nude photo of herself and texts it to the principal, does that make him in possession of child pornography? An assistant principal in Virginia was convicted on that charge but later cleared his name in appeals court.

Teenage boys are notorious for not thinking things through before they act. Boys in Indiana and Ohio have been indicted on charges of obscenity or contributing to the delinquency of other minors for sexting cases involving photos.

What about text messages exchanged between consenting adults? The U.S. Supreme court is considering a California case where a man used his company-owned pager to text his wife and his mistress. The suit alleges that the company violated the man's privacy after reading the thousands of messages. The case is still pending.

Texting and Driving

If a driver runs over a pedestrian while texting, was that the cause of his negligence—and can he be charged with manslaughter? A California case thought so in 2009. All over the U.S., states are instituting laws that make it illegal to use a cell phone for any purpose while driving, unless it's a hands-free setup.

Enforcing the law is somewhat problematic, and fines for texting and driving are minimal. In Virginia, for instance, people pulled over on suspicion of drunk driving who were found to only be texting pay a $20 fine, and the minor charge is often dropped if other violations are found.

A more recent case in Missouri alleges that a 16-year-old girl committed manslaughter when she crashed into a great-grandmother and killed her. The teenager was certified to stand trial as an adult and is awaiting trial.

Texting Laws and Implications

Overall, the new technology of SMS text messages is causing many twists in court cases all over the nation. Is texting just another wrinkle in complex cases, or is it the direct cause of bad behavior and poor decision-making?

The implications of these cases are important for.

Sexting

The slang word "sexting" is a combination between "sex" and "texting," and it's a sticky subject among cell phone users. While most of the uproar centers around teenagers, adults have also gotten into trouble when sexy messages, photos or videos make their way out of private conversation into the public.

Sexually suggestive text messages range from flirting to all-out booty calls, from mildly offensive to downright pornographic. As with any intimate conversation, sender and receiver must both be willing participants for sexting to remain harmless, and there is always the danger that one or the other will show an outsider what was said and reputations will be damaged.

Sexting Among Teenagers

Various studies have found that anywhere from 15 percent to 60 percent of teenagers have sent or received explicit images or messages via text. Cell phone cameras make snapping a photo easy;

text conversations can quickly get heated as messages fly back and forth.

Sexting certainly happens and, as more children own cell phones, the prevalence of sexually suggestive text messages is on the rise among young people. Technology makes it easy to say and do unacceptable things, and the impact seems more acceptable because conversations aren't in person.

A vast majority of texts between teens are completely innocent as they carry on teenage conversations about everything in the world. Sexting is something to watch for in peer groups and catch as early as possible before it escalates into hurtful behavior.

Sexting among Adults

Politicians, movie stars, singers, athletes and business leaders have fallen victim to sexts becoming public. It seems humans enjoy a juicy bit of gossip, and the permanent proof of words and photos on the smartphone screen lends credibility to lurid claims.

Regular adults have found trouble in racy text messages, too. It's much harder to hide an affair when a thousand flirtatious texts are waiting to be read in someone's cell phone. And, it's easy to pose as someone else when phone numbers are the only thing identifying people in the conversation.

It is possible to use text messaging to spice up a legitimate relationship. Sexting should be done by agreement between consent- ing adults who have a relationship of trust between them. Even then, messages should be deleted when the conversation is over to avoid the possibility of an outsider reading them.

Sexting: It's Part of the Culture Now

Adults who send text messages may be able to avoid inappropriate behavior, but the temptation will always be there to flirt with a spouse or partner at the very least. Parents of teenagers probably don't need to panic; sexting is yet another wrinkle in young people's lives that should be talked about.

Establish boundaries with others and be clear about what you will and will not do via text message. If you're OK with mild sex- ting, you might find it fun and interesting!

CHAPTER 2

STOP WASTING MONEY ON EXPENSIVE ADVERTISING

There's no question that technology changes the face of everything we see and do today, including marketing and advertising. Traditional print ads, billboards and commercials cost small business owners thousands of dollars and are never guaranteed to touch your specific target market. Today, cell phone marketing is on the rise and fast becoming even a customer's preferred way to receive notification of sales and specials at their favorite businesses.

Lucky for small business owners, text message marketing is one of the most affordable ways to personally reach loyal and preferred customers on a regular basis. For low monthly subscription fees, you send unlimited messages to your list of opted-in customers advising them what's new and improved with your business.

It seems nearly everyone on the face of the earth has a cell phone today, and they take advantage of TMM from businesses they visit on a regular basis. Cell phone marketing is much more targeted and successful than traditional marketing methods, where you throw everything against the wall and "see what sticks."

Over time, you'll learn which types of messages are the most cost-effective and beneficial for your business. You'll never send spam because these customers have chosen to receive your messages (opted in with their cell phones), but you also don't want to overwhelm them, either.

For less than the cost of a small classified ad in the weekly paper, you can send as many messages as you'd like. Most businesses utilize the genius of TMM once or twice a month, and may segment their customer lists into more specific categories.

Once you take a look at your advertising and marketing costs from last year, you'll realize how affordable TMM can be as an effective marketing method for even the smallest businesses. Start utilizing cell phone marketing today and let your customers know how savvy you've become.

CHAPTER 3

TEXT MESSAGE MARKETING

So, you've created your text message marketing account. Wasn't that easy? Now, you're excited to communicate with your prospects. Take a step back before sending any TMM messages and develop a plan of attack so your SMS marketing messages work together as a strong advertising campaign.

Create excitement for special events. Beginning a month or more before the big day, text your TMM customers that something great is coming up and you'll give them more details soon. This creates curiosity and interest. Your next TMM message should tell them a little more but still not everything. A week before the big day, reveal everything they need to know so they can mark their calendars. Finally, send one last reminder text message that now it's time!

Capitalize on slow business cycles by creating specials exclusively for your TMM prospects. For instance, text your customers a deal that's good only between the hours of 10 a.m. and noon on Tuesday. Vary the days and times each week, and choose a new special frequently. Offer them something they can't resist and your mobile text customers will come running even in slow times.

Look outside your business for more opportunities to contact your customers via text. Community events are a great time to invite customers to your business. A quick "Stop by after the parade and enjoy an appetizer" would work well for a restaurant, for instance. A car dealership could offer a free test drive to anyone coming from an afternoon at the auto show. Music festival-goers might enjoy a cocktail at your bar and lounge, especially if you've got a band playing later. Motivational speakers could build a database of interested prospects from the audience who want to purchase products. Be creative and find ways to link events with your business.

Balance your cell phone marketing efforts between the predictable offers and the surprise deals. Regular customers love knowing they can count on your business to always offer something great, and surprise deals catch the interest of customers who visit your business less frequently. You don't always have to offer TMM prospects something free, but do give your customers a good reason to read your TMM messages.

The key with any marketing campaign is to touch your customers often enough to keep their interest without overloading them so they opt out of your TMM list. Even the most faithful customers will get tired of hearing from you if you text them too much. Make sure the text messages are timely and worthwhile for your prospects, and plan ahead so all your messages present a focused marketing campaign

CHAPTER 4

USE TEXT MESSAGE MARKETING TO BRING IN REPEAT BUSINESS

Did you know that every one of your customers is lying in wait for the next big deal to come along? It's high time you reached them with innovative marketing strategies like TMM, also known as text message marketing or cell phone marketing. Let your preferred customer base know about deals as they happen. TMM reaches them faster than any television or radio commercial, billboard or print advertisement can.

Every time someone shops at your store, places an order by phone, or visits your website, ask if they would like to be placed on your TMM list. This way, you are constantly adding to your database of customers who prefer cell phone marketing methods.

Research has shown that cell phone marketing is one of the best ways to reach customers today on a personal level, so ensure you're business is ready to move forward and put TMM to work for you. Although some merchants are leery of trying text message marketing, it's fast becoming the most popular way to both send and receive marketing information. Your customers opt in with their cell phones to receive promotional text messages from you. They can easily opt out with a quick text reply if they don't want to hear from you any longer.

Cell phone marketing works for retail stores of all sizes and kinds, restaurants, spas and health clubs, and all businesses that depend on a large and growing customer base to stay afloat and thrive in a declining economy. Stop missing out on repeat business by staying in touch via cell phone marketing. These little advertisements gently remind your customers why they do business with you in the first place

CHAPTER 5

SURROUND YOUR BUSINESS WITH LOYAL CUSTOMERS

C ustomers become loyal because they find quality in your service or product and feel that they benefit from it. Unfortunately, your competition is also trying to win over the same small set of customers to create a presence in the market. The secret is to use creative marketing methods such as TMM, or text message marketing, to establish a personal connection with your customers and turn them into loyal repeat buyers.

TMM allows you to show your customers you're watching out for them. Giving them exclusive notice of sales, events and special pricing that the general public doesn't know about definitely makes them feel as if they must take advantage of the opportunity.

What's more, cell phone marketing is not only convenient for your customers but targets those who are most likely to take advantage of the event itself. Placing an ad in the newspaper, posting a billboard on the road, or filming a television commercial may or may not draw additional traffic to your event—these forms of marketing depend upon the right people seeing them at the right time. With TMM, you're always targeting those most likely to be there.

Over time, using text message marketing allows you to build a strong relationship with customers and thus increases referrals and your repeat business. It is far easier and cheaper in both time and money to gain repeat sales from your current customer base than it is to find brand new customers.

Utilizing your marketing dollars wisely through cell phone marketing techniques is by far the most economical and simplest way to create a loyal customer base and thus ensure the long-term success of your business. Subscription fees are low compared to most other forms of advertising.

Every type of business depends upon sales and customers to stay afloat. Establishing repeat customers and referrals through text message marketing is the easiest way to ensure your continued success long-term. TMM works—put your customers' cell phones to good use to promote your business.

CHAPTER 6

MAKE YOUR CUSTOMER AN OFFER THEY CAN'T REFUSE

In today's tough economic times, it's sometimes hard to secure loyalty from current customers. Everyone knows that sales create income, and numbers create sales. Unfortunately, not every type of marketing is effective and targeted directly to your current customers.

Text message marketing (also called TMM or cell phone marketing) is a great way to reach customers on a personal level and increase response from marketing efforts. They opt-in to receive text messages from your small business, so you're never sending them spam. With a targeted message about special pricing, events or hours, you'll find that these tiny ads result in more sales and bigger crowds than expensive newspaper, radio, or television ads.

Make sure you're offering customers and potential customers deals they can't refuse. This may mean that net profits per sale are lower, but your market share will definitely grow if you give it enough time. By undercutting the competition through either price or extra offers, you'll find that your business grows during slow times and comes out on top when the market recovers, too.

If you're a small business that can't under price your product, influence customers through free giveaways and other specials. Offer free kid's meals on certain days with the purchase of each adult entrée, or offer free tripods with the purchase of a camera.

You choose cell phone promotions that add value to customers and bring them in the door.

Feel free to be as creative as possible, and remember that you may be one of the first to try TMM in your business niche. The competition has no idea you're even using text message marketing, let alone what you're offering and how often. This is a huge advantage to you as a small business owner.

Track response to your cell phone marketing efforts and you'll notice that some messages spark a noticeably larger crowd than others. Take these cues as free advice about what to keep and what to get rid of in future text messages. Remember to stick with what works and continue to offer similar deals to your customers, and you'll have no problem surviving virtually any economic climate

CHAPTER 7

HOW TO WRITE TO THE POINT TEXT MESSAGE MARKETING MESSAGES

Congratulations! You've decided to take the next step in becoming a modern and technologically smart small business by using text message marketing (TMM). You're saving money on advertising, increasing your customer base, and experiencing a higher return on your investment. Now, you simply need to hone your skills at writing these magical messages.

First, determine the purpose of your cell phone text message. Are you inviting the customer to a special event? If so, simply give the title of the event, date and time, and maybe one sentence about the purpose. If you plan on holding a grand re-opening to show off your remodeled store, say just that and tell them when to show up. A lengthy story about how and why you remodeled will simply turn customers off and reduce your turnout.

In other cases, you may use cell phone marketing to let customers know about special deals and pricing. Since your TMM list only contains customers who have opted in, they already know why you're sending them a text message. Simply title your message, "Deals This Friday Only, 05/14," add a brief list of items, and finish up with the new, reduced prices. There's no need to cram any more information into these types of messages.

In today's technological age, everyone's into cell phone marketing for ease of use and how incredibly fast TMM works. Don't forget that your customers are extremely busy and are more likely to skip over or delete your text message if they feel it's too lengthy or not worth their time. Let's be real – you do the same thing with marketing emails when they show up in your inbox, too.

If you've ever received a text or email from anyone under the age of 50, you know that everyone understands universal symbols and acronyms. Don't hesitate to use these in your text messages, either. Always remember to only tell them what they must know, and you'll find your TMM efforts blossoming throughout your business.

Creating Events through Text Message Marketing

As a small business owner it's sometimes hard to generate new and fresh ideas to keep your customers' interest and get them excited about visiting you on a regular basis. When you start to feel the slump of lowered sales and miss the crowds knocking down your door, it's probably time to establish your own buzz in the marketplace.

Text message marketing, also known as TMM or cell phone marketing, is a fresh and welcome way for you to touch your customers on a regular basis. You ask them to opt-in to your TMM list with a quick text message, and let them know they can opt out just as quickly if they don't want to receive promotional text messages from you. It's not spam—it's helpful information delivered where they need it, when they need it, via cell phone text message.

TMM is so incredibly simple and effective you'll wonder why you ever spent thousands on TV or radio commercials, or edited endless creative for a newspaper ad, or ever lamented a slow day for your small business. Running a commercial or classified advertisement will not only give the competition a heads-up on what you're planning, but you have no way to track your return on investment.

When you use cell phone marketing, within moments you target your best customers with short text messages about special pricing or sales, early bird specials, or even an exclusive invitation to a customer appreciation open house. No matter what type of event you choose to create, the secret is to text as many targeted customers as possible. Cell phone marketing is the perfect way to make sure you're reaching the right people. These customers are more likely to participate in the event you've created because they've opted in to your TMM list, letting you know they trust you and want to spend their money with you.

Another great way to increase response is to ask your opted-in customers to invite their friends and family via text messages. If you create an event that simply can't be ignored, they'll naturally tell everyone they know and bring you more business than you could have imagined.

Text message marketing can be used on a regular basis to not only maintain your connection with your most loyal customers, but also to generate interest in continuing to do business with you in the future. When the competition is struggling, text message marketing helps you create your own reason for celebration.

CHAPTER 8

HOW TO TRACK YOUR TEXT MESSAGE MARKETING EFFORTS

Next message marketing is one of the most affordable ways for you to stay in touch with your loyal customer base and advertise upcoming special events. How do you know if your messages are effective? Don't just look at sales numbers in general and guess at increased response to TMM messages. Track customers carefully to gauge the effectiveness of cell phone marketing.

Cell phone marketing is extremely effective, but you must have a concrete plan and stick with it. First, determine what you're using the TMM for. Do you want to increase sales overall, or increase repeat business from loyal customers? Are you hoping for higher online sales, or greater response to special events and open houses? You know your business priorities and if you have more than one priority, TMM makes split testing incredibly easy.

Find a way within the message itself to track response to TMM. Will recipients be given exclusive access during hours you aren't typically open? Will they order a special entrée that isn't on the regular menu? Give them a coupon code to use at checkout whether online or in the store. These simple promotions give you a clear picture of whether they're taking advantage of your offers or not.

If you find that certain cell phone messages tend to flop and others turn out a huge crowd, discern the differences and stay with what works. For example, your TMM may offer a sale price on a certain item that flies off the shelf in 24 hours. On the other hand, you may invite customers to an open house and end up with a gallon of coffee and three dozen cookies to share with your employees. Cell phone marketing results tell you that customers are looking for deals and not necessarily a chance to mingle or see what's new in your establishment.

Always track how many text messages you're sending and how many sales or visits you receive as a result. Distinguish between online, telephone, and in-person sales to track which place of commerce your customers prefer. This tells you how to further utilize your cell phone marketing attempts in the future.

Unadvertised Bonus

The Ultimate IM Dictionary

Contents

Click on an alphabet below to navigate:

A

A/B TESTING - The method in marketing research to test the effectiveness of marketing strategies. A/B testing starts with a control or initial marketing scenario. The control scenario 'A' is usually defined through several aspects (e.g. cost, color, texture, shape, fonts, site layout, web copy etc). An alternative scenario 'B' is created by changing the defined aspects. Subsequently, the market response from 'A' will be compared to that of 'B'.

ABOVE THE FOLD - The section of a Web page that is visible without scrolling. Ads placed above the fold are assumed to be viewed and clicked more often. Therefore, advertisers often look favorably at placements that are above the fold on a Web page.

AD BLOCKING- The blocking of Web advertisements, typically the image in graphical Web advertisements. There are claims that download time improved considerably by blocking slow-loading banners and buttons. Consequently, ad blocking might actually encourage more aggressive forms of generating revenue. If legitimate Web advertising is eliminated, content sites will feel the pressure to sacrifice editorial integrity by using sneaky advertorials, charge subscription fees for content... or be forced out of business.

AD COPY- The actual text in an advertisement that aims to get your prospective customer's attention and get you more clicks and sales.

AD SPACE- The space on a Web page available for advertisements. Ad space is now a major factor for sites that are dependent on advertising revenues. One of the challenges of Web design is to use ad space in a way that delivers for advertisers without alienating visitors.

AD TRACKER- A tool or software that you can use to track and measure the ROI (Return On Investment) of your marketing methods including links, pay-per-click campaigns, autoresponders, affiliates, popups, banners, salescopy, articles, reports, ebooks, and even offline ads.

ADSENSE - A program by Google that you can use to add advertisements to your websites and make money when visitors to your websites click on the posted advertisements.

ADVERTISERS - People or businesses that place advertisements on publishers' sites to promote their product or service with the intention to get sales or visits.

ADWORDS - A pay-per-click advertising program by Google that you can use to advertise your website and products, and only pay when your advertisement is clicked on.

AFFILIATE- Someone who gets paid a commission or reward for referring a paying customer to a merchant's site.

AFFILIATE MARKETING- A marketing strategy which involves revenue sharing between online advertisers/merchants and online publishers/salespeople. Compensation is based on performance measures, typically in the form of sales, clicks, registrations, or a hybrid model. Affiliate merchants are the advertisers/merchants who want to sell their products. Affiliates are the publishers/salespeople who market or promote the products of the affiliate merchants through various methods.

Some examples of affiliate merchants include:

☐ Amazon.com

☐ Clickbank.com

☐ Commission Junction

AFFILIATE SOFTWARE- A software that provides tracking and reporting of commission- triggering actions (sales, registrations, or clicks) from affiliate links.

Affiliate merchants use affiliate software to handle transaction tracking and reporting. These software costs range from free and almost-free scripts to expensive software packages.

ALEXA- A website that rates other websites on the Internet based on their popularity. Available at www.Alexa.com

ALT TEXT- A HTML attribute that provides alternative text when non-textual elements, typically images, cannot be displayed.

ANONYMOUS FTP- An option in FTP that allows users to download files without having to establish an account. Anonymous FTP, sometime shortened to Anon FTP, is often used for large files of public archives.

Apache- An open source web server software. Apache is found primarily on Unix-based operating systems, but is also available for Windows and other platforms.

ARTICLE MARKETING- A type of advertising whereby you submit articles to article directories and include your resource box, so that you can generate free traffic to your website and increase your site's page rank.

AUTORESPONDER- A program that automatically responds via email to people who sign up for your newsletters, ecourses, ezine etc. You can also pre-set the program with several email messages to be sent to your subscribers at predetermined time. An example of a powerful and reliable autoresponder service is Aweber which can be found at

http://www.aweber.com

B

B2B- Business that sells products or provides services to other businesses.

While business-to-business activity exists both online and offline, the acronym B2B has primarily been used to describe the online variety.

B2C- Business that sells products or provides services to end-user consumers.

While business-to-consumer activity exists both online and offline, the acronym B2C has primarily been used to describe the online variety.

BANDWIDTH- The amount of space allocated to you by your hosting service to be used by visitors to your website. Each visitor to your website uses a number of bytes when they open your webpage, and each month, you only get a fixed number of bytes.

BANNER ADVERTISING- A network of website owners that agree to barter or exchange banner advertisements displayed on their websites using a pre-agreed exchange rate.

BANNER BLINDNESS- The tendency of web visitors to ignore banner ads, even when banners contain information visitors are actively seeking.

BASIC RESELL RIGHTS- These rights allow you to sell the product you purchased to others but those that bought this product from you are not allowed to sell it.

BEYOND THE BANNER- Online advertising which does not involve standard GIF- and JPEG-format banner ads.

Beyond the banner is crucial to create some differentiation in online advertising. This is because banners have become so common that it makes it easy for Web surfers to ignore the banners.

BLOG- A form of online journaling which involves frequent, chronological publication of personal thoughts and Web links. A blog is often a mixture of what is happening in a person's life and what is happening on the Web. Some examples of blogging sites:

- Blogger.com

- Wordpress.org

- Livejournal.com

Blogs are also called web logs or weblogs.

BOOKMARKING- Social bookmarking is a new way to advertise your website by adding a link to your website at social bookmarking sites where people will be able to see them. It is an effective way to get traffic to your website.

BOUNCE RATE- In web analytics, bounce rate is the percentage of visitors who leave after viewing a single page. In email marketing, bounce rate is the percentage of emails in a campaign that are undeliverable.

In web analytics, bounce rate is used to describe the effectiveness or ineffectiveness of a particular web page.

BUM MARKETING- A marketing method coined by Travis Sago that uses article marketing to promote affiliate links and sites. You basically choose an affiliate product, get your affiliate link, write articles to promote it, and then submit the articles.

BUSINESS PLAN- A series of steps listing all your goals and what you need to do to achieve success in your business.

C

CALL TO ACTION (CTA)- A part of the marketing message that attempts to persuade a person to perform a desired action.

A call to action aims to persuade a visitor to perform a certain act immediately. Some common examples of CTAs are "Buy Now!" and "Register Today!" The call to action is intended to improve the market's response rate to the ad copy, as its absence may cause a visitor to forget about the ad and move on to other things.

CACHING- The storage of Web files for a later re-use, at a pace more quickly accessed by the end user.

The objective of caching is to make efficient use of resources and speed up the delivery of content to the end user.

CAPTCHA- abbrev. "Completely Automated Public Turing test to tell Computers and Humans Apart". It is a challenge-response testing system whereby the reader must re- type in a given field, a series of ambiguated characters shown by an image.

CAMPAIGN- All the work involved with promoting and advertising a particular website, product, or service.

CAMTASIA- A popular video-making software that is especially useful for making screen capture videos to show what you are doing on your computer. You can get the software from www.techsmith.com

CLICKBANK- One of the most popular online marketplaces that focuses on and sells digital products such as e-books and software; you can also get affiliate links to these products to promote them and make money. You can check out the site here:

http://www.Clickbank.com

CLICK-THROUGH RATE (CTR)- The average number of click-throughs per hundred ad impressions, expressed as a percentage.

The CTR may be seen as a measure of the immediate response to an ad, but not the overall response to an ad. This is because visitors may have seen an ad but instead of clicking through, they may go directly to the URL.

CONTEXTUAL ADVERTISING- A method of serving advertisements based on the content (i.e., overall context or theme) of a web page.

Google AdSense was the first advertisement service that introduced the inclusion of a page's overall context in determining which type of ad campaigns will be rolled out for that page.

CONVERSION RATE- It tells you how many visitors to a website actually become customers. For example, if you are getting 1 sale for every 100 visitors to your website, then you have a 1% conversion rate.

COOKIE- Preferences information stored on a user's computer by a Web.

Cookies are passed from a Web server through a Web browser to the user's hard drive. This information is essential for many of the features on the Web, such as shopping carts and personalized portals.

COPYWRITING- The use of words and text to promote a person, business or product. It is commonly used for advertisements and other marketing materials to persuade the reader to act (eg. to buy a product). Here's an excellent course on copywriting:

CPANEL- It is the control panel of your website provided by web hosting services that enables you to login and manage your files as well as other information related to your website.

COST-PER-ACTION (CPA)- Online advertising payment model in which payment is based solely on qualifying actions such as sales or registrations.

The actions defined in a cost-per-action agreement relate directly to some type of conversion, such as sales and registrations. This does not include transactions based solely on clicks, which are referred to specifically as cost-per-click or CPC.

COST PER CLICK (CPC)- The amount of money you have to pay whenever someone clicks on your advertisements, links, or text when you use an ad-buying program.

COST PER THOUSAND IMPRESSIONS (CPM)- The CPM model refers to advertising bought on the basis of impressions.

The total price paid in a CPM deal is calculated by multiplying the CPM rate by the number of CPM units. For example, 100,000 impressions at $10 CPM equals a $1,000 total price.

CSS- It is the acronym for Cascading Style Sheets and it is now commonly used to style webpages instead of HTML. A webpage can have many different CSS, each controlling the look of part of the page and one CSS that combines everything and bring the entire webpage together.

D

DATA TRANSFER- The total amount of outbound traffic from a website (excluding email), typically measured in gigabytes (GB).

Data transfer is often confused with another term – bandwidth. The difference between bandwidth and data transfer is that bandwidth is a rate and data transfer is a total.

Note: Many hosts use the terms bandwidth and data transfer interchangeably, referring to a monthly data allowance as bandwidth.

DEDICATED HOSTING- A type of hosting where a portion of space on the hosting company's servers is allocated exclusively to you for your domain or site. Hostgator has reliable dedicated servers and is a great choice for hosting your sites. Sign up for

Hostgator here: http://www.hostgator.com

DEDICATED IP- An IP address dedicated to a single website.

Dedicated IP addresses are mainly needed for SSL. To avoid the risk of being caught up in an IP ban, search engine optimizers tend to prefer dedicated IPs. Regardless of whether this is a real or perceived risk, many webmasters would rather be safe than sorry.

DEEP LINKING- Linking to a web page other than a site's home page.

Some argue that deep linking unfairly eliminates the ability of the home page to contribute to brand building and ad serving functions.

DIRECT LINKING- It means placing a link for an affiliate program in an advertisement, article, or some other form of advertisement leading visitors to the merchant's site. This is not as effective as leading visitors to a intermediary landing page that pre-sells the affiliate product.

DIRECTORY- A web directory groups links to websites into categories and displays them, making it easy for people to find websites that interest them. Placing a link to your website at web directories is also a way to get back links.

DOMAIN NAMES- It is the name of your website and is made up of a series of alphanumeric strings separated by periods. Example of domain names are: internetmarketing.com, internetmarketing.net, internetmarketing.org... You can register for a domain name at www.Namecheap.com or www.Godaddy.com

DOORWAY PAGE- A web page made specifically to rank well in search engines for particular keywords. It serves as an entry point through which visitors pass to the main content.

E

E-COURSE- A series of online lessons or e-mails that teaches or provides you with information on a specific topic. In other words, it's a course that is conducted over the Internet.

EMAIL MARKETING- A form of marketing whereby you use email to send sales letters and newsletters to your subscribers/customers to promote a service or product. It is now commonly used in home-based business and commercial industries because it is much more cost-effective compared to traditional printed direct mail, and also because subscribers can instantly receive the emails.

EXCLUSIVITY- The contract term in which one party agrees to grant another party sole rights with regard to a particular business function.

This is often seen in some advertising networks which demand exclusivity. Others which do not demand exclusivity offer a higher rate for an exclusive deal than the standard rate given to non-exclusive deals.

EZINE- It means electronic magazine and is basically an online magazine.

EZINE DIRECTORY- Directory of electronic magazines, typically of the email variety. Ezine directories are like catalogues that list the different available electronic magazines online. They often organized into high-level categories similar to other general Web directories. Once you find the ezine directory best suited to your needs, don't let it go.

F

FACEBOOK- A social networking site located at facebook.com.

Facebook is the largest social networking site in the world, with 750+ million active users as of July 2011. Following its rise to popularity, marketers can utilize this site to reach people by using direct Facebook advertising or by non-advertising avenues (social media marketing and/or content marketing).

FANTASTICO- A script installer that is run on many web hosting accounts and usually accessible from cPanel. It enables you to easily install blogging, content, carts and other popular scripts on your website, by only clicking a button.

FAVICON- A small icon (typically a logo) that is used by some browsers to identify a bookmarked Web site.

Favicons are most used by large, well-branded sites such as portals and media companies. These little custom icons are used to make a website bookmark more prominent in a long bookmark list.

The display size of a favicon in the Favorites list is 16x16. Files are recognized by the ".ico" extension.

FLASH- A popular way to add content to a websites as the pictures, graphics and words are often moving and colorful, making them interactive and also visually interesting for visitors.

FORUM- An online meeting place for people with common interests to exchange views and ideas on a particular topic.

FORWARDING- Resending an e-mail from your e-mail inbox to another email address.

FRAMES- A structure that allows for the dividing of a Web page into two or more independent parts.

Frames are often used to keep one or more parts of a Web page static while another part of the page is scrolled or loaded. Benefits can include faster page loading and the ability to keep a navigation bar present on the visible part of the page.

FREQUENCY CAP- Restriction on the amount of times a specific visitor is shown a particular advertisement.

Frequency capping is used to avoid banner burnout so that visitors are not being overexposed causing response to drop. This method is effective for campaigns of a direct- response nature measured by click-throughs. However, it defeats the purpose of campaigns targeting to build a website's/company's branding.

FTP (FILE TRANSFER PROTOCOL)- A way of transferring files from your computer to your website or vice versa. You usually have to use some kind of software such SmartFTP, a free FTP software, to do it.

<u>G</u>

<u>GEO TARGETING</u>- A method of detecting a website visitor's location to serve location- based content or advertisements.

A website visitor's location can be detected by the computer's IP address. The first three digits of an IP address corresponds to a country code, while the succeeding digits often refer to specific areas within that domain.

<u>GIVE AWAY RIGHTS</u>- These rights enable you to give the product away for free.

<u>GOOGLE CHECKOUT</u>- An online payment system powered by Google.

Google checkout enables users to save their credit card information in their Google account so that they can quickly perform online purchases in participating sites, without needing to manually enter credit card information every time.

<u>GOOGLE INSTANT</u>- A feature of Google's search engine that shows instant search results as the keyword query is being typed.

For search marketers, Google Instant has the potential to funnel more traffic towards phrases suggested by the system, and short-circuit some of the natural long-tail search activity.

GUERILLA MARKETING- A form of online marketing using unconventional methods and is sometimes viewed as unethical because of certain techniques used. It aims to get the greatest possible profits from the most minimal amount of resources.

GUEST BLOGGING- Writing a blog post to be published on another blog as a temporary featured author.

GURU- A person that is an expert in a certain area or has had remarkable success in that area, and uses their knowledge to guide others.

<u>H</u>

<u>HEATMAP</u>- A graphical representation of data where varying degrees of a single metric are shown using colors.

A very powerful tool when preparing website navigation and sales copy, heatmaps are often used by online marketers to evaluate the most-used parts of a web page. It can be via eyetracking, clicktracking, mousetracking, etc. Results of most viewed parts of the page are often displayed with dark red, with less viewed parts displayed as lighter red, orange, yellow, etc.

<u>HITS</u>- The number of file requests for your website where even images and index page also count as single hits. It is not a good way to measure the amount of traffic to your website.

<u>HOME PAGE</u>- The main page of a Web site.

The home page can be said to be the most important page of a Web site. This is because visitors who arrive at a slow-loading or poorly-designed home page may not view the rest of the site. They might even decide to avoid the site in the future. Therefore, home pages should be designed intricately to be fast-loading and intuitive.

HOSTING- An online place that holds all the files for your websites as well as provides you with bandwidth, the amount of space that you can use, and database accounts. You can get cheap and reliable hosting at www.Hostagator.com

HTML- It is the acronym for Hypertext Markup Language and is the code used to define webpages. You can use it to define the look of text, buttons, banners, and other components of your webpages.

HYBRID MODEL- A combination of two or more online marketing payment models. A hybrid campaign might be a mix of CPM, CPC and CPA; or a mix of CPC and CPA models. Hybrid deals are sometimes seen as a way to further split the risk between publishers and advertisers.

I

IM- It is the acronym for Internet Marketing and means marketing products or services online to make money.

IMPRESSION- It is the number of times your link appears on another website and is often used in Adwords to show how many times your ads are displayed.

INBOUND LINK- A link that directs people to your website.

INCENTIVIZED TRAFFIC- Visitors who have received some form of compensation for visiting a site.

Incentivized visitors typically do only what is necessary to gain the incentive and nothing more. Incentives may come in the form of cash, points, or other means. While incentivized clicks/traffic is the most notable incentive-based action, other forms exist such as incentivized registrations.

INBOUND MARKETING- A marketing model whose sales performance relies on the initiative of its client base to find and purchase a product.

Inbound marketing is best described as a passive sales model. Unlike outbound marketing, a buyer should make the "first move" before any promotional tactics are used.

<u>INTERSTITIAL</u>- An advertisement that loads between two content pages.

Interstitials are a form of interruption marketing. One of the most common interstitials is the pop-up ad. Another emerging format is a full-page ad that interrupts sequential content, forcing exposure to the advertisement before visitors can continue on their content path.

J

JAVASCRIPT- A type of programming language used in web pages to give it interactive components and it is usually shorter and more powerful than coding only in HTML.

Tip: JavaScript is good if you want shorter code but when Google ranks your website, it will not be able to read it as content.

JOINT VENTURE (JV)- It means working together with another marketer to make money. Both parties make certain agreements and follow them through till the end of the agreement term.

<u>K</u>

<u>KEYWORD DENSITY</u>- Keyword density is the percentage of times a keyword or phrase appears on a web page compared to the total number of words on the page. In the context of search engine optimization, keyword density can be used as a factor in determining whether a web page is relevant to a specified keyword or keyword phrase.

<u>KEYWORD RESEARCH-</u> The act of finding keywords that are searched for often in search engines but have little competition. Here's a superb keyword research software:

<u>KEYWORDS</u>- The word or phrase that you are trying to target for a particular website, web page, or article, and it is also the actual word or phrase people type into search engines. An example is "dog training".

<u>KEYWORD MARKETING</u>- A form of marketing involving putting your message in front of people who are searching using particular keywords and phrases.

For ad buyers, keyword marketing involves purchasing ad units, typically banners, on the search results page when a Web surfer searches for particular keywords and phrases. For search engine optimization professionals, keyword marketing involves achieving top placement in the actual search listings.

KEYWORD STUFFING- The excessive, unnatural use of keywords on a web page for search engine optimization purposes.

KEYWORDS TAG- META tag used to help define the primary keywords of a Web page. The keywords tag belongs in the <HEAD> section of a Web page, typically placed below the META description tag. Keyword tags are additional information to the website content. Do not use any keyword excessively, as search engines will perceive this as spamming. Also, keep the keywords and phrases relevant to the actual text of the page.

L

LANDING PAGE- The page between your advertisement or article and your merchant's website. This page usually contains a review of the merchant's products or a testimonial for the merchant.

LINK EXCHANGE- It means swapping your link with others. They then display your link on their sites, and you post their link on your website.

LIKE-GATE- A barrier requiring a user to "Like" a brand's page before they can access certain content from that brand on Facebook.

Like-gating is a marketing effort by brands on Facebook to increase their Fans more quickly than they would otherwise. Marketers use great offers to persuade people into becoming fans on a Facebook fan page. This concept is similar to "email subscribers" and "permission marketing".

LINK BUILDING- The process of increasing the number of inbound links to a website in a way that will increase search engine rankings.

Link building is a process to improve a page's search ranking for a given keyword or keywords. A page's rank (generally) improves by increasing the number of incoming links, whose corresponding anchor text is relevant to the targeted keyword(s).

LINK CHECKER- Tool used to check for broken hyperlinks.

Link checking is one aspect of site management -- the regular maintenance necessary to keep a site up-to-date.

A "broken hyperlink" refers to a link that does not correctly point to the intended destination page. A hyperlink is "broken" when the destination page is deleted or moved to another location.

LINK POPULARITY- A measure of the quantity and quality of sites that link to your site. Link popularity is under the off-page criteria of search engine optimization. It is used to determine quality content. Off-page criteria of search engine optimization adds the aspect of impartiality to search engine rankings, as citations from other authors in the Web community helps define a site's reputation. In theory, great sites will naturally attract many links, and content-poor sites will have difficulty attracting any links.

LINKBAIT- A piece of content deliberately created with the primary purpose of attracting inbound links.

In the earlier days of the web, site owners noticed that certain types of content generated an inordinate amount of inbound links, especially from the blogosphere and influential sites like Digg. That gave rise to a flood of content that was increasingly formulaic, the most blatant of which spurred the name linkbait.

LINKEDIN – LinkedIn.com is a business-related social networking site. Founded in December 2002 and launched in May 2003, it is mainly used for professional networking. As of 22 March 2011, LinkedIn reports more than 120 million registered users, spanning more than 200 countries and territories worldwide.

LINKROT- When Web pages previously accessible at a particular URL are no longer reachable at that URL due to movement or deletion of the pages. (broken links)

LIST- In email marketing, it refers to a database of people who are interested in your market or niche and have signed up with you. The information is usually stored in your autoresponder service.

LIST BUILDING – the process of adding subscribers/customers to your database.

LOG FILE- File that records the activity on a Web server.

Log files generate information such as which files are requested, when files are requested, who requested them, and where they were referred from.

M

MANUAL SUBMISSION- Adding a URL to the search engines individually by hand. Manual search engine submission may be more time consuming than automated search engine submission, but a fair amount of optimization specialists stick with the "old fashioned way."

MARKETING PLAN- The part of the business plan outlining the marketing strategy for a product or service.

The marketing plan includes information such as the product or service offered, pricing, target market, competitors, marketing budget and promotional mix.

There is off-the-shelf software to guide entrepreneurs through the formulation of a business plan. Some sites also offer sample business plans to emulate for added guidance.

MAILING LIST- A group of all the people who have willingly given to you their email address, and you can at any time send emails to these group of people telling them about products and services you are promoting.

MERCHANT- The seller of a product or service, and you are trying to get people to buy from the seller so you can make money.

META SEARCH ENGINE- A search engine that displays results from multiple search engines. Not all search engines are metasearch engines. In non-metasearch engines, there may be primary listings and secondary listings. The secondary listings serve as a backup to enhance the search coverage... or as a premium (paid) service to enhance the search engine's revenue. These additional listings may or may not be clearly distinguished as being outside the primary results.

META TAG- A part of your HTML code contains information describing your web page, and this part of the code is often displayed in search engine results.

MINI-SITES- They are something like landing pages but contain more information about the product, service, niche, or merchant at the site. You would typically have about 4-5 pages of related information and this increases the amount of information you have for Google to scan, which might result in a higher Page Rank for your site.

MODERATOR- In a forum, specific people are given the power to watch over and regulate what other people at the forum post, and if something breaks the predefined forum rules, a moderator can delete the post and/or ban the person who posted the content from the forum.

MOUSETRAPPING- The use of browser tricks in an effort to keep a visitor captive at a site, often by disabling the "Back" button or generated repeated pop-up windows.

Mousetrapping is one of the most extreme marketing tactics on the Web. The goal is to extract maximum value from one-time visits, typically by bombarding visitors with a never-ending supply of traffic-exchange banners and pay-per-click links.

Master Resell Rights (MRR)- These rights allow you to sell the product and also give the person who bought the product its resell rights. This means that the person you sell to can also sell the product if you allow them to do so.

MYSQL- An online database that is included with your web hosting package. It gives you the ability to maintain a database through your web host storing information such as customer logins, the way they like their web pages to be displayed, etc.

N

NAVIGATION- That which facilitates movement from one Web page to another Web page.

Clear and user-friendly navigation is often taken for granted, but it plays a crucial role in getting site visitors to view more than just the home page. If navigation choices are unclear, visitors may elect to hit the "Back" button on their first (and final) visit to a Web site. Once they enter, the real challenge begins, as it is no easy task to allow first-time visitors to get take maximum advantage of a site.

NETIQUETTE- Short for network etiquette, the code of conduct regarding acceptable online behavior.

NEWBIES- This refers to people who are new or inexperienced at something.

NEWSLETTER- This is an online publication that you email to a list of people who signed up for it. It can contain information related to the reason why they signed up for it.

NICHE- A specialized subset of a market comprising of a group of people with interest in a specific area that you want to target and promote to. An example would be:

<u>NICHE RESEARCH</u> – The process of researching profitable niches to market to.

<u>O</u>

<u>OPTIN</u>- This is when a person signs up to be in your mailing list. Double opt in is when the person will have to confirm his subscription through e-mail as well.

Tip- Double opt in helps you ensure that your subscriber provided a working email.

<u>OPT-OUT</u>- (1) type of program that assumes inclusion unless stated otherwise. (2) to remove oneself from an opt-out program.

Opt-out is sometimes used to refer to email which assumes inclusion; sometimes having "Yes" automatically checked on a signup form, sometimes by adding your name directly to a list. (Although in the latter case the term email spam is often used.)

The terms opt-out and unsubscribe have subtly different, yet related, meanings. You unsubscribe to something to which you had previously subscribed. You may opt-out of something you never joined in the first place.

<u>ORGANIC SEARCH</u>- The unpaid entries in a search engine results page that were derived based on their contents' relevance to the keyword query versus all the other indexed content on the web. With the introduction of features like Google OneBox & Universal Search, the organic search results are not as simple as ten ordered text listings. Now

THE BUSINESS TEXT MESSAGE CONNECTION

the free side includes things like videos, images and product listings, giving site owners multiple opportunities to get more "organic" exposure.

OUTBOUND LINK- A link to a site outside of your site.

Outbound links send visitors away from your web site. Attitudes towards outbound links vary considerably among site owners. Some site owners still link freely. Some refuse to link at all, and some provide links that open in a new browser window.

The con of outbound linking is that it risks losing time and money from site visitors. This can be a large risk if a site is facing high customer acquisition costs.

OUTSOURCING- Getting other people and paying them to do work such as writing your web pages, articles, ads, and sales pages for you. You can also get them to do any other things that you think it is easier to pay others to do than doing it yourself.

P

PAGE VIEW- Request to load a single HTML page.

Page views are only important to the degree they play a part in a site's revenue model. If a site earns much of its revenue from advertising, then page views are important because of their contribution to ad inventory. If a site only earns revenue on sales, then page views are not a key statistic. Page views without corresponding sales may even be viewed as an expense.

PAGEJACKING- Theft of a page from the original site and publication of a copy (or near- copy) at another site. Pagejacking does not mean taking over a page on the original site. In fact, the original site can be completely unaware that the theft has occurred.

PAY PER SALE (PPS)- Online advertising payment model in which payment is based solely on qualifying sales. Advertiser only pays when sales are generated by the destination site based on an agreed upon commission rate.

PAYPAL- A service that allows any individual or business with an email address to send and receive payments online securely, easily and quickly. It supports 190 countries and regions around the world. You can visit its website here: www.Paypal.com

PAGE LOADS - It is the number of times your page has been accessed and is a popular way of counting the number of people that visited your site, but it is not as good a way as counting the number of unique visitors.

PARALYZATION- It is something which is experienced by most newbies and is something like information overload. It means that you have read so much information that you do not know where to start and what to do next.

Tip- All you need to do to get over your paralyzation is to focus and choose to do one thing at a time.

PAYMENT THRESHOLD- Many websites that pay you commission or a fixed fee enforce this and it is the minimum amount of money that you have to earn from them before you will get the actual money.

PDF- It is an acronym for Portable Document Format and it is a file format by Adobe. This is the most popular file format used for ebooks.

PHP- It is a scripting language that is mainly used to create dynamic web pages, allowing you to add different interactive elements on your website. It is mostly used on Linux servers or hosting servers.

PLR- It is the acronym for Private Label Rights and it means you can sell, modify, split up, and/or put your own name and links in the product unless stated otherwise.

PRIVATE MESSA (PM)- These are little messages that you can receive or send to other people in forums or using other applications. It is something like an email between you and the other person without both of you having to actually exchange email addresses.

PODCAST- A series of audio or video files that are syndicated over the Internet and stored on client computing devices for later playback.

POP-UNDER AD- An ad that displays in a new browser window behind the current browser window. The pop-under ad is the sneakier relative of the pop-up ad. While pop- up ads are often shown (and closed) instantly, pop-under ads linger behind the current browser window, appearing only after other windows have been closed.

POP-UP AD- An ad that displays in a new browser window.

Pop up windows come in many different shapes and sizes, typically in a scaled-down browser window with only the Close, Minimize and Maximize commands.

PORTAL- A site featuring a suite of commonly used services, serving as a starting point and frequent gateway to the Web (Web portal) or a niche topic (vertical portal).

PAY PER CLICK (PPC) — This refers to a payment scheme where you have to pay whenever someone clicks on your ads, or links.

PAY PER LEAD (PPL) – This refers to a payment scheme where you pay someone or a company whenever a lead is generated for you.

PAGE RANK (PR)- This is a number assigned to your page by Google search engine and it is a measure of its importance on the Internet. Check your page rank here:

PRE-SELL- Pre-selling means you giving a personal review or testimonial for a product or merchant. By doing so, you are telling potential customers more about the product, its good and bad, and so remove any doubts they have before directing them to the merchant's site.

PRESS RELEASE- It is an announcement to the public with respects to the who, what, where, when and why of a topic. It can include things like what is new, what is going to happen, etc. An example PR site – www.PRWeb.com

<u>PUBLISHERS</u>- These are people who allow advertisers to place advertisements and links on their web pages, and in return for it, they get paid by the advertisers.

R

RECIPROCAL LINKS- These are the links that you have that points back to directories or any other sites, in return for them displaying a link to your website on their sites.

REDIRECTING- It means automatically transferring visitors from one site to another site. Usually you transfer people from a site with a shorter URL to one with a longer URL so that visitors only need to type a shorter address to get to your site and can remember it better.

Tip- This is the code of a redirect link:

<head>

<meta HTTP-EQUIV="REFRESH" content="0;

url=http://www.dwaynewhiting.com/">

</head>

RESELL RIGHTS- These rights allow you to sell the product but you can pass the sell rights to customers. This means that the person who bought the product from you cannot sell it.

RESOURCE (BIO) BOX- A small area of text that you get when submitting articles which is used to place details about you, your website or product.

Tip: The more interesting you make your bio box, the more likely people will click the link to visit your site.

RETURN DAYS - The number of days an affiliate can earn commission on a conversion (sale or lead) by a referred visitor.

If an affiliate program offers 45 return days, commissions are earned for conversions completed any time within 45 days of the initial click-through on the affiliate link. The visitor may later go directly to the merchant's site and not visit the affiliate's site again, as software is used to track the visitor's origin.

RSS- Acronym for Really Simple Syndication. It is a feed of posts or information at your site. When someone signs up to get it, they receive notification via their reader whenever your site is updated with new content.

RUN-OF-SITE- Ad buying option in which ad placements may appear on any pages of a target site.

S

SALES COPY- It is the information written on your sales page aimed at getting visitors attention and eventually for them to purchase your product or service.

SALES LETTER- It is a letter to the customer aimed at getting them to purchase your product or service. It can contain information such as product description, benefits, price, testimonials, etc. Otherwise known as sales page or sales copy.

SCRIPTS- Small portions of code that allow web browsers to perform interactive and dynamic tasks such as allowing you to move widgets, enabling you to add items to shopping cart, countdown product quantity, and many more.

SEARCH ENGINE- A program that indexes documents, then attempts to match documents relevant to a user's search requests.

A search engine powers the search process and provides results for a search destination.

Web search engines attempt to index a large portion of pages on the World Wide Web. Other search engines are topic-specific, region-specific, and even site-specific.

SEARCH ENGINE OPTIMIZATION (SEO)- The process of designing, building, and promoting a website with the search engines in mind..

SERPs-It is the acronym for Search Engine Results Page, and it is the page that is returned when you search for a keyword in search engines. The page displays all the results returned for your keyword.

SEARCH ENGINE SUBMISSION- The act of supplying a URL to a search engine in an attempt to make a search engine aware of a site or page. When submitting to search engines, sometimes additional contact information, including name and/or email address is needed for consideration.

SEARCH RETARGETING- The use of a site visitor's search history as a basis for the ads that the visitor will see. For example, suppose a search engine user regularly searches for terms like "clean", "energy" and "environment" for a couple of hours. With this data, ad providers like Google AdWords or Yahoo! Marketing can serve ads about sustainable living and environmental protection.

SERVER- A computer or computer program that manages access to shared resources in a network of computers.

SEARCH SPY- A perpetually refreshing page that provides a real-time view of actual Web searches. While not as immediately useful as keyword databases that summarize monthly totals, search engine spies can give insight into how people actually search. Search engine spies come in filtered and unfiltered varieties.

SKYSCRAPER AD- An online ad significantly taller than the 120x240 vertical banners. Skyscraper ads are tall with standard sizes of 120x600. The wide skyscraper is 160x600. These types of ads are often called skyscraper banners, although some examples have mimicked the look of a banner by using a combination of ad buttons

SHARED HOSTING- It means that all the websites are located on one server and each has a different part in the server so that they are separated.

SHOPPING CART- Software used to make a site's product catalogue available for online ordering, whereby visitors may select, view, add/delete, and purchase merchandise. Shopping carts are available as standalone software or as part of hosted storefronts.

Here's an example of a shopping cart:
http://www.2checkout.com/

SIGNATURE (SIG)- Usually in forums and e-mail, you can insert your own signature at the end of the message. You can place information to promote your product, website, or any other information that is within the forum rules.

SITE BUILDER- It is a software that you can use to easily create your website instead of coding it with HTML from scratch. You can use the software to help link all your web pages, add images and text to your content, and many more.

SITE SEARCH- Search functionality specific to one site.

Site search can make or break the user experience. Great search results can help win long-time visitors. Poor search results ("no records found" or "every record found") risk losing visitors forever.

SOCIAL BOOKMARKING- Social bookmarking is a new way to advertise your website by adding a link to your website at social bookmarking sites where people will be able to see them. It is an effective way to get traffic to your website.

SPAMMING- This means sending unsolicited emails to a large number of people. Another form of spamming is when you post a large number of unrelated messages at forums just for getting traffic to your website.

THE BUSINESS TEXT MESSAGE CONNECTION

SPLASH PAGE- A branding page before the home page of a Web site.

Splash pages are usually graphic-intensive pages that appear before the main home page. Some feature standard graphic format such as GIF and JPEG; others feature formats such as Macromedia Flash that require a special plug-in (which a visitor must download if he or she does not already have one).

SQUEEZE PAGE- A web page specially designed to obtain the email address of visitors. To do so, you can offer people a free gift, discount, etc so that they will sign up and give you their email address.

STICKINESS- The amount of time spent at a site over a given time period.

Stickiness is often measured in the average minutes per month visitors spend at a site or network. Sometimes stickiness is measured in terms of page views.

When defined as minutes per month, site stickiness is a function of number of visits (repeat usage) and time spent per visit (session stickiness).

SUBDOMAINS- These are websites that are part of your main website. For example, in the domain imlovebirds.com a subdomain could be blog.imlovebirds.com

SURROUND SESSION- Advertising sequence in which a visitor receives ads from one advertiser throughout an entire site visit.

SUPER AFFILIATE- An affiliate capable of generating a significant percentage of an affiliate program's activity. A super affiliate might account for more results than hundreds or thousands of smaller affiliates combined. Partnering with a super affiliate allows affiliate managers to spend less time on administrative duties and more time on generating results.

T

TEMPLATE- A predefined file that contains common images or headers that are required for a website or advertisement, which you can just use by adding in your own details. This way, you do not have to create everything from scratch each time you need to create a similar website or advertisement.

TEXT AD- Advertisement using text-based hyperlinks.

Text-based ads, although common in email, have been dominated on the Web by their graphical-based counterparts.

TEXT LINK EXCHANGE- Network where participating sites display text ads in exchange for credits which are converted (using a predetermined exchange rate) into ads to be displayed on other sites.

TITLE TAG- HTML tag used to define the text in the top line of a Web browser, also used by many search engines as the title of search listings.

A title tag belongs in the <HEAD> section of a Web page, above the <BODY> section.

TRACKING CODE- Many affiliate programs use this to relate sales to the affiliate marketer. They do so by putting small pieces of code in an affiliate link so that they know who to credit the sale to when purchase are made via that link.

TRAFFIC- It is the amount of visitors to your website. Driving traffic means actively finding ways to get more visitors to a website. The more visitors you get, the more sales you are likely to have.

TRUE COMPETITION- The actual competition your website faces. To find out your true competition, search with quotes around your target keywords and the results returned are those websites that target exactly the same keywords as you do.

TURNKEY SITES- These are websites that have everything set up for you. All the text, images, tables, headers, and links are already set up at the website and ready for you to use. You just need to get traffic and also may have to add your own tracking code to the links.

TWITTER – Twitter.com is an online social networking and microblogging service that enables its users to send and read text-based posts of up to 140 characters, informally known as "tweets", and images. Here's a program that puts your Twitter marketing on steroids! http://twittenator.com

<u>TWO-TIER AFFILIATE PROGRAM</u>- Affiliate program structure whereby affiliates earn commissions on their conversions as well as conversions of webmasters they refer to the program.

U

UNIQUE VISITORS- It is the number of different people to your website. The people are identified by their IP, which is their Internet address. You can use a tool to find out how many unique IPs there are to your website and can also customize how often the unique IPs are counted.

UNDERDELIVERY- Delivery of less impressions, visitors, or conversions than contracted for a specified period of time.

Underdelivery can occur for a variety of reasons. A site or network may experience an unexpected drop in traffic. Low CPM campaigns may be bumped for high CPM campaigns.

URL- Location of a resource on the Internet.

A URL, short for universal resource locator, includes the protocol (ex. HTTP, FTP), the domain name (or IP address), and additional path information (folder/file).An example URL: http://dwaynewhiting.com

USABILITY- The ease with which visitors are able to use a Web site.

Web site usability is about how quickly and easily visitors are able to make use of the site. Usability is a concern for marketers because of its potential impact, positive or negative, on marketing metrics such as conversion rates, which in turn affect profitability.

V

VIRAL MARKETING- A marketing method that depends on people to share information promoting a product or service to all of their friends quickly.

VERTICAL BANNER- A banner ad measuring 120 pixels wide and 240 pixels tall. According to the IAB (Interactive Advertising Bureau), vertical banner specifically refers to a banner ad measuring 120x240. Technically, there are other banner ad sizes that are also vertical in nature. Skyscrapers ads, for instance, are significantly taller than wide, but they have their own specific name.

VLOG- A blog that publishes video content; a video blog.

Vlogs surged in popularity with the advent of broadband (a.k.a. high-speed) internet, which allowed real-time viewing of video content.

VOLUNTEER DIRECTORY- A Web directory staffed primarily by unpaid volunteer editors.

W

WEB 2.0 - A term often used to describe the ongoing technological change on websites that provide high-technology web-based applications to end users. Web 2.0 websites are generally sites where visitors are able to submit and control content. An example of Web 2.0 site is YouTube.com.

WEB BROWSER- A software application that allows for the browsing of the World Wide Web. Eg: Internet explorer, Mozilla Firefox etc

WEB DESIGN- The selection and coordination of available components to create the layout and structure of a Web page.

Web design has a significant impact on Web marketing efforts. Factors like how visitors find the site (search engine optimization), how long visitors use the site (site stickiness), how likely visitors are to return (repeat visitors) and how often visitors buy or register (conversion rate).

WEB DIRECTORY- Organized, categorized listings of Web sites.

The terms "Web directory" and "search engine" are often used interchangeably. Web directories are organized Web site listings put together by human reviewers, whereas search engine listings are put together by automated systems and lack a navigable structure. Much of the confusion stems from the various hybrid models that have developed over time, as search engines have incorporated directory features to assist with

WEB RING- A means for navigating a group of related sites primarily by going forward and backward.

Web rings are large-scale grassroots phenomena made up primarily of small/midsize sites. The number of web rings and member sites runs into the millions.

WEB SITE TRAFFIC- The amount of visitors and visits a Web site receives.

Web site traffic was initially viewed as an all-important metric for gauging success on the Web. Now profitability is the focus, and Web site traffic is only part of the equation. Web site traffic x conversion = results

Web site traffic is still important, as you can't have conversions without visitors, but it is becoming less important as a standalone metric.

WHOIS- A website that enables you to find out who the owner of a domain is, where it is hosted, and contact information of the owner.
http://www.networksolutions.com/whois/index.jsp

WORD-OF-MOUTH MARKETING- A marketing method that relies on casual social interactions to promote a product. A person is more likely to believe something that comes from a person that he knows or respects, instead of a canned source like commercials and print ads.

WORDPRESS- A popular website and script that is used for blogging. This website is different from others as it enables you to posts as well as pages to your blog. You can download Wordpress here: http://www.wordpress.org

WSO- Warrior Special Offer- If you are a member of WarriorForum (http://www.WarriorForum.com/forum), you can offer other members a special price for a product or service you are selling and this is known as WSO. You need to be a member of the War Room plus pay $40 per listing, and additionally the special price you are offering has to be only for members of WarriorForum and not to the public.

www.ingramcontent.com/pod-product-compliance
Lightning Source LLC
Chambersburg PA
CBHW071246170526
45165CB00003B/1257